metal clay

RINGS

silver jewelry
inspired by nature

irina miech

KALMBACH BOOKS

Kalmbach Books
21027 Crossroads Circle
Waukesha, Wisconsin 53186
www.Kalmbach.com/Books

Published in 2010
14 13 12 11 10   1 2 3 4 5

Manufactured in the United States of America

ISBN: 978-0-87116-278-6

Publisher's Cataloging-in-Publication Data

Miech, Irina.
  Metal clay rings : silver jewelry inspired by nature / Irina Miech.

    p. : col. ill. ; cm.

  ISBN: 978-0-87116-278-6

1. Precious metal clay—Handbooks, manuals, etc. 2. Rings—Design—Handbooks, manuals, etc.
3. Jewelry making—Handbooks, manuals, etc. 4. Silver jewelry—Handbooks, manuals, etc.
I. Title. II. Title: Rings

TT212 .M54345 2010
739.2782

contents

introduction

Throughout history, rings have had a special significance among jewelry. With no beginning and no end, their shape evokes infinity, endlessness, and the continual cycle of life.

A ring is worn on the finger for all to see. It may promise a lifelong vow or send a message of power. Rings are often talismanic, considered to have special powers or great spiritual meaning.

Engagement rings and wedding rings are among the oldest and most well-known examples of the symbolism of the ring. Ancient Egyptians, Greeks, and Romans used wedding rings to identify a woman as being married. Originally made of braided reeds or herbs, rings were carved of bone or wood and later made of metal as people craved more permanent symbols.

Wearing a ring on a specific finger may communicate special meaning. High-ranking officials wore their rings on the index finger because that finger was considered the most powerful. The fourth finger or "ring finger" is thought to have a connection to the wearer's heart, and, in Western culture, wearing a ring on the fourth finger of the left hand usually signals that the wearer is betrothed.

Today, whether meaningful token or a fanciful fashion statement, rings are a common accessory for men and women alike. *Metal Clay Rings* will teach you how to make your own.

about this book

The incredible medium called metal clay enables more people than ever before to create their own rings and other jewelry.

In this book, I share techniques for making some of my favorite rings. If you make each project in the order presented, you'll build a foundation of ring-making skills as well as a jewelry box full of beautiful metal clay rings.

Each project also includes gallery photos of creative extensions of the techniques. It is my wish that you'll finish this book equipped with skills and inspired with ideas for designing your own new and unique jewelry.

Anna Miech

6

creating
metal clay rings

Making rings is unlike creating any other metal clay object. Issues of sizing, form, and wear and tear come into play as you shape your metal clay rings.

Metal clay shrinks as it is fired. Because rings need to fit snugly around a finger—or may even need to fit a particular finger—you'll want to consider size and shrinkage as you shape your rings.

When I make rings, I always use PMC3, the third-generation formula of silver clay, because its composition makes it the strongest and densest of all the metal clays after firing. The equivalent in Art Clay brand is ACS 650.

Many factors affect shrinkage, including clay type and ring width, thickness, and shape. Wherever there is more volume of clay, there will be greater shrinkage. In a ring that has a wide and a narrow side, the wider side will shrink more than the narrower side. Also, adding volume to the ring (by adding embellishments, for example) will cause that area to shrink slightly more.

It's best to start your ring two sizes larger than the desired finished size. If the ring has a seam, allow extra clay for the overlap at the seam. It's very important to make strong seams and reinforce them well. Using a ring form during firing will help prevent shrinkage past the desired size and will also prevent distortion.

I make rings thicker than other metal clay projects because rings are subjected to more wear. Usually I roll my clay to 5 cards (1.25 mm) thick for rings. I fire rings for two hours at 1650°F (900°C) for maximum strength and durability. I recommend using a digitally programmable kiln because it's the only way to hold that precise temperature for two hours (many teaching facilities offer kiln use or firing services).

Polishing rings in a rotary tumbler or magnetic polisher work-hardens them, increasing their strength and durability.

Ring shank shapes

When a ring has two parts, a band that encircles the finger and a decorative element attached to the band, the band is often referred to as a *shank*. Shaping the shank by rolling, trimming, and forming the metal clay is often the first step in any ring project. Here are a few ideas for shapes:

SIMPLE BAND Parallel edges form a simple, elegant band, often seen in traditional wedding rings.

HOURGLASS Use this shape to make a band that's wider at the front and narrower in the back. Some people find this style more comfortable to wear.

TRIANGLE Cut a long triangle of clay to create an asymmetrical, contemporary ring.

In the projects, you won't find a specified length for the clay strip that forms the ring shank. The length depends, in part, on the finished size of the ring you're making. Here's a general guide:

Finished size	Length
Up to size 5	2¹⁄₂ in. (64 mm)
Sizes 6–8	2³⁄₄ in. (70 mm)
Sizes 9–11	3 in. (76 mm)
Sizes 12–14	3¹⁄₄ in. (83 mm)

ring-making
tools

If you'd like a short refresher on many of the basics of working with metal clay, please see the chapter at the end of this book. This section spotlights key tools and techniques that are specific to making rings.

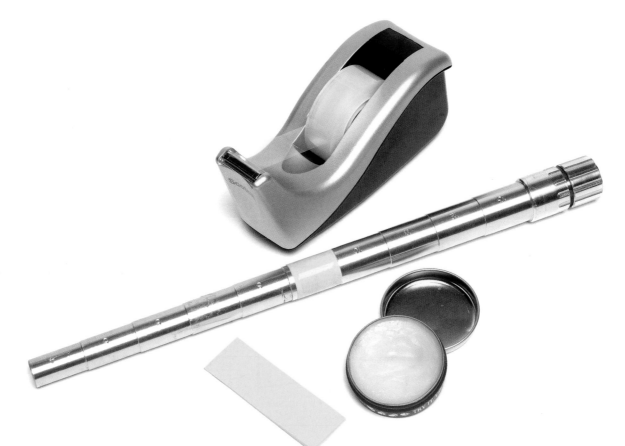

Many of the projects call for a **ring mandrel setup**. Here's what you'll need: On a stepped steel ring mandrel, wrap a sticky note at the step two sizes larger than the desired size. Wrap the note with clear tape. Grease the tape lightly with balm or oil; usually you'll let the ring dry on the mandrel, and greasing the tape helps the ring release easily. A stepped mandrel is better than a tapered mandrel, which can distort the ring size (especially if you're making a wide band).

The **RingMaker**, a relatively new tool from Japan, is a mold set designed specifically for making uniform ring bands. In several projects, I use it to make flat and half-round seamless bands. To use the mold, lightly grease the parts that will come into contact with clay, insert a lump of clay, and punch out the center. You can buy specific sizes of molds that correspond to the ring sizes you plan to make.

Use a metal or plastic **ring-sizing gauge** to determine a desired finished ring size. Most gauges include full and half sizes.

Fire your metal clay ring around a **ring form** to control shrinkage and prevent distortion. Forms are made out of casting investment; you can purchase them in full and half sizes. Each form is used only once. After the ring is fired (and cool, if it has stones), soak the ring and the form in a cup of water for a few minutes (don't use the cup for anything else). The casting investment will soften; remove it underwater and dispose of it following the instructions from the manufacturer.

project tools & supplies

Many projects call for items from a basic metal clay toolkit—tools that are essential for working with metal clay. Keep the entire kit at your work table or check the project for a list of the specific items that you'll need. (Projects also list any additional tools needed.) Here's the full list of items in my basic toolkit:

- balm or oil
- drinking straws
- needle stylus
- paintbrush with small "bright" tip
- plastic mat
- playing cards
- roller
- rolling rectangle
- ruler
- sanding pad
- scalpel
- toothpicks
- tweezers

Projects often call for a mandrel setup (see p. 8), a kiln setup (see Kiln Firing, p. 94), and a tumbler setup (see Polishing, p. 94). Read up on all of the basic tools, materials, techniques, and equipment in Metal Clay Basics, p. 91.

river
stones

Start with a fine-silver ring blank to make this quick and easy ring.

This ring evokes a river bed, its pebbles polished by time and water.

1 Paint the ring blank with a thin coat of oil paste. Let dry overnight.

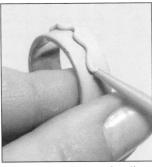

2 Decorate with curving lines of syringe clay.

materials

Fine-silver ring blank
PMC3 syringe clay
Art Clay oil paste
Fine-silver casting grain

tools & supplies

From basic toolkit: tweezers
Paintbrush dedicated to
    oil paste
Kiln setup
Tumbler setup
Liver of sulfur and polishing
    pad (optional)

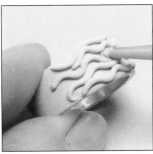

3 To add silver casting grain, first make a tiny syringe blob.

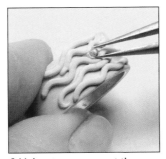

4 Using tweezers, set the casting grain on the blob, and push it all the way in. Continue to add casting grain as desired between the lines.

5 Let dry. Fire and tumble-polish the ring. Use liver of sulfur to add patina if desired.

● Oil paste takes a long time to dry. You'll need to
● let the coated ring blank sit at least overnight.
●

variations

The simple band can be embellished in many exciting ways—CZs in settings, casting grain, and stamped or molded shapes.

A fine-silver band made in the same way became the bezel setting for this large CZ pendant. Dots of syringe clay hold the stone in place.

wrapped
leaf

Learn the basics of shaping clay around a ring mandrel.

This simple ring conveys nature's perfection in a single leaf shaped into an endless band of silver.

1 Prepare the mandrel: Wrap the sticky note around the mandrel at the step that is two sizes larger than the desired finished size. Wrap the tape all the way around the sticky note. Grease the tape liberally.

• • •
materials
PMC3 clay (8–10 g)
PMC3 syringe clay

tools & supplies
From basic toolkit: balm or
    oil, paintbrush, plastic
    mat, playing cards, roller,
    ruler, sanding pad, scalpel
Large leaf
Mandrel setup: steel ring
    mandrel, sticky note,
    clear tape
Kiln setup
Tumbler setup
Liver of sulfur and polishing
    pad (optional)

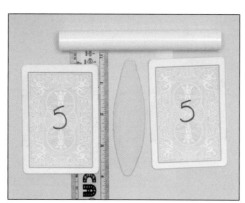

2 Roll the clay to 5 cards (1.25 mm) thick, occasionally stopping to shape it with your fingers into a tapered shape as shown. Roll to 4 in. (10.2 cm) long.

3 Place the clay on the back of the leaf where the veins are most prominent. Roll to 5 cards.

• Look for a leaf with
• well-defined veins.

4 Remove the clay from the leaf. Trim it with the scalpel into a tapered leaf shape about 3½ in. (89 mm) long.

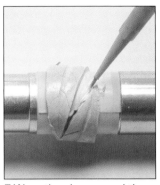

5 Wrap the clay around the prepared mandrel. Apply syringe clay to the seam where the ends will meet.

6 Join the ends. Apply additional syringe clay to reinforce the seam.

7 Smooth the seam with the paintbrush. Let the ring dry on the mandrel.

8 Remove the ring from the mandrel and reinforce the inside seam of the ring with syringe clay.

9 Spread the clay evenly with the paintbrush. Let dry.

10 Sand the inside of the ring with a flexible sanding pad.

11 Fire and tumble-polish the ring. Use liver of sulfur to add patina if desired.

variations

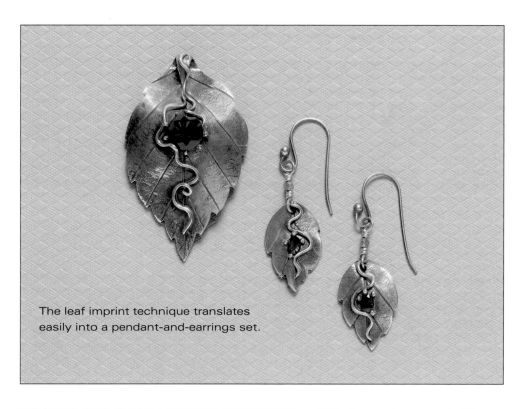

The leaf imprint technique translates easily into a pendant-and-earrings set.

I set a large, oval CZ in rings of syringe clay to give the Wrapped Leaf ring an entirely different look.

simplicity

*Use the RingMaker tool to shape three classic half-round bands
that can be worn separately or stacked.*

This simple yet elegant ring is a beautiful example of the symbolism of an endless band, which has no beginning and no end.

1 To prepare the RingMaker mold, use balm or oil to lightly grease the cylinder and the inside of the base and top. Roll the clay into a ball about 1 in. (26 mm) in diameter. Flatten the ball slightly.

2 A good size for the flattened ball is slightly larger than the center opening in the base. Place the clay over the opening.

● ● ●

materials
PMC3 clay (starting amount, 16 g; actual amount used, 4 g)
PMC3 paste
2 mm CZ

tools & supplies
Half-round RingMaker mold set
From basic toolkit: balm or oil, paintbrush, plastic mat, sanding pad, scalpel, tweezers
Kiln setup
Tumbler setup
Liver of sulfur and polishing pad (optional)

3 Place the top over the base and press the two parts together firmly. Use your fingers to force the clay into all parts of the ring-shaped space.

4 Insert the cylinder in the center of the mold, pressing down with your index fingers. Use your thumbs to keep the mold closed.

●
● The acrylic mold components can be damaged by
● heat, so it's best to let the ring air-dry.

5 Push the cylinder all the way through the opening. (Preserve the plug of clay for use in another project.) Remove the top part of the mold slowly with a slight twisting action. Let the ring dry in the mold at least overnight.

6 Remove the dry ring from the mold.

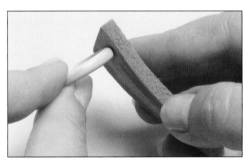

7 Sand the ring.

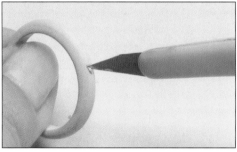

8 Using the point of the scalpel in a twisting motion, drill a hole in the ring. Drill through to the inside of the ring, making the hole wide enough on the outside of the ring to hold the 2 mm CZ.

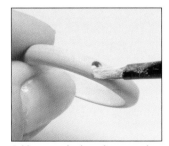

9 Use a paintbrush to apply a small amount of paste to the inside of the hole.

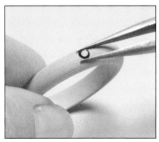

10 Using tweezers, carefully place the CZ in the opening.

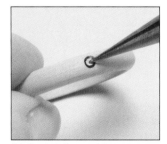

11 Push it in, making sure the girdle (widest part) of the CZ is below the surface of the clay. Let the paste dry.

12 Fire and tumble-polish the ring. Use liver of sulfur to add patina if desired.

variations

A RingMaker band accented with stamped leaves and syringe-clay vines forms the loop of this lariat.

You can join two or more bands made with the RingMaker. Casting grain accents the seams of this ring.

forest
jewel

Mold a twig to get started on this unusual setting for a large CZ.

A single gem, framed by tree branches, is the focal point of this forest-inspired ring.

materials
PMC3 clay (6–8 g)
PMC3 syringe clay
Oval CZ or lab-created
 corundum, 6 x 8 mm

tools & supplies
Small twig (about 3 in./
 76 mm long)
From basic toolkit: balm or
 oil, drinking straw,
 paintbrush, plastic mat,
 rolling rectangle, ruler,
 sanding pad, scalpel,
 tweezers
Two-part molding compound
Ring mandrel setup: steel
 ring mandrel, sticky note,
 clear tape
Kiln setup
Tumbler setup
Liver of sulfur and polishing
 pad (optional)

1 Prepare the mandrel. Mix two-part molding compound until the color is uniform. Shape it to accommodate the twig. Press the twig into the mold compound.

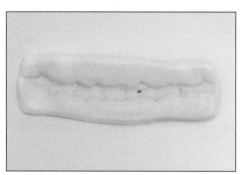

2 When the mold is set, carefully remove the twig. Lightly grease the mold.

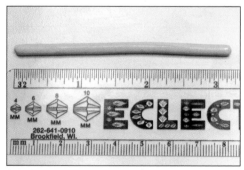

3 Roll a snake about 3 in. (76 mm) long.

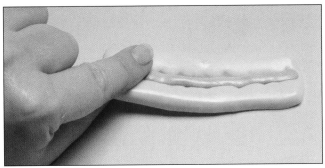

4 Gently press the clay snake into the mold (avoid pressing hard in the center).

5 Lift the clay out of the mold and wrap it around the mandrel as shown, leaving a gap of about ⅜ in. (10 mm) for the setting. Trim and remove any excess clay. Let dry on the mandrel.

6 Roll a small piece of clay into a ball about ⅜ in. (10 mm) in diameter. Slightly flatten and elongate the ball.

7 Squeeze the drinking straw lightly to create an oval opening and punch it through the clay.

8 Using tweezers, set the stone on top of the clay and gently push it in.

● As you take walks in nature, collect twigs and
● other interesting forms to use with metal clay.

9 Let the gem setting dry.

10 Sand the shank with a flexible sanding pad. You may want to remove some texture on the sides and back for a comfortable fit.

11 Sand the gem setting.

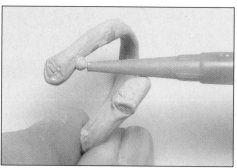

12 Add syringe clay to the points where the setting will attach to the shank.

13 Attach the setting. Let the ring dry.

14 Use syringe clay to reinforce the join and embellish the ring.

15 Let dry. Fire and tumble-polish the ring. Use liver of sulfur to add patina if desired.

This free-form variation is a molded twig shape with syringe-clay flourishes.

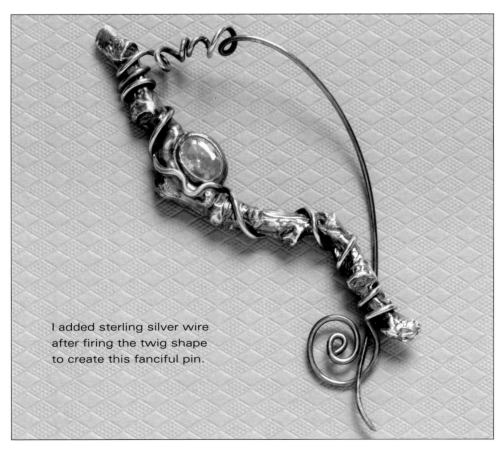

I added sterling silver wire after firing the twig shape to create this fanciful pin.

autumn
leaves

*Learn how to shape a basic hourglass shank and embellish it
with tiny shapes and texture.*

This ring reminds me of walking through swirling leaves on a crisp fall afternoon.

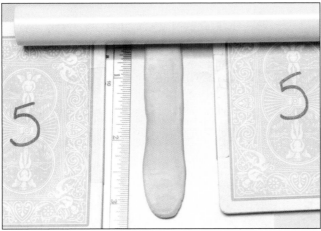

1 Prepare the mandrel. Roll the clay 5 cards (1.25 mm) thick to about 3 in. (76 mm) long and at least ½ in. (13 mm) wide.

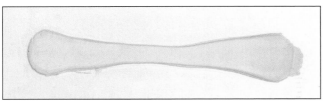

2 Cut an hourglass shape that's about ½ in. (13 mm) at its widest point.

3 Wrap the clay around the mandrel, overlapping the ends. With the scalpel, cut through both layers of clay to create a butt join. Remove the excess clay from both ends.

4 Strengthen the seam: Blend and intermingle the clay from both sides using the tip of the scalpel.

● ● ●

materials
PMC3 clay (6–8 g)
PMC3 syringe clay
Fine-silver casting grain

tools & supplies
From basic toolkit: balm or oil, paintbrush, plastic mat, playing cards, roller, ruler, sanding pad, scalpel, tweezers
Vintage brass stamping
Half-round file
Mandrel setup: steel ring mandrel, sticky note, clear tape
Kiln setup
Tumbler setup
Liver of sulfur and polishing pad (optional)

● The hourglass shank
● is the foundation
● of many of the ring designs in this book.

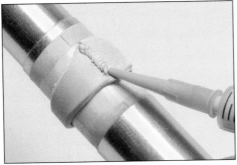

5 Apply a line of syringe clay to reinforce the seam.

6 Smooth with the paintbrush. Let the ring dry on the mandrel.

7 Use syringe clay to fill the seam on the inside of the ring.

8 Smooth the seam with the paintbrush and let it dry.

9 Using a flexible sanding pad, smooth all surfaces of the ring.

11 Cut out the leaf shapes (they do not have to be perfect). Make as many shapes as you want. (My ring has six leaf shapes.)

12 To curve the leaves, place them on the prepared spot on the mandrel. Let all the leaf shapes dry on the mandrel.

10 Prepare another spot on the mandrel: Wrap a sticky note, add tape, and grease it. Roll a small amount of excess clay to 3 cards (.75 mm) to create small leaf components. Press the clay into the brass stamping.

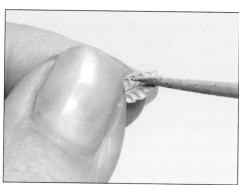

13 Smooth the leaf shapes with a flexible sanding pad. Use a half-round file to shape and define the edges.

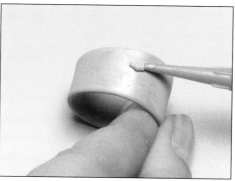

14 Apply an elongated blob of syringe clay to the band. This will attach the first leaf component.

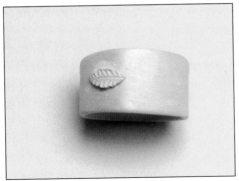

15 Attach the leaf components to the front of the ring with syringe clay. Leaves can touch each other and overlap.

16 Add some wavy lines of embellishment with syringe clay.

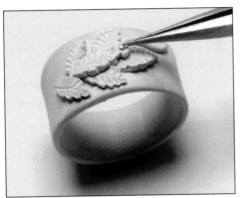

17 Attach small casting grain pieces with syringe clay.

18 Let dry. Fire and tumble-polish the ring. Use liver of sulfur to add patina if desired.

Stamped flowers, each with a center CZ, are a cheerful springtime substitute for leaves.

This simple pendant with a rolled bail uses the same stamped leaf shapes as the Autumn Leaves ring.

burst of
beads

Use needle and thread to embellish a screen base with bright crystals.

Make this playful ring your own with sparkling crystal beads in your favorite colors.

1 To create the shank, follow steps 1–6 of the Autumn Leaves project, p. 26. Before the clay dries, use the clay cutter to punch a hole through the center of the ring directly over the seam. (If the seam tears, repair it with syringe clay.)

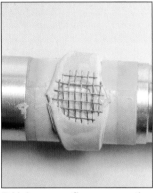

2 Using your fingers, gently curve the screen to follow the shape of the ring. Place it over the hole and gently press it into the clay.

● ● ●

materials
PMC3 clay (6–8 g)
PMC3 syringe clay
1 g charlottes (size 13 or 15)
25–30 4 mm crystal bicones
Beading thread
G-S Hypo Cement
Brass screen, ½ in. (13 mm) square

tools & supplies
From basic toolkit: balm or oil, paintbrush, plastic mat, playing cards, roller, ruler, sanding pad, scalpel
Clay cutter (³⁄₈ in./10 mm)
Scissors
Beading needle
Mandrel setup: steel ring mandrel, sticky note, clear tape
Kiln setup
Tumbler setup
Liver of sulfur and polishing pad (optional)

3 Using syringe clay, make dots around the edge of the screen to secure it. Smooth with the paintbrush. Let dry on the mandrel.

4 Remove the ring from the mandrel. On the inside of the ring, fill in and repair the seam using syringe clay.

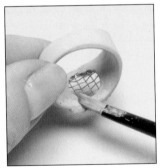

5 Smooth with a paintbrush if needed. Let dry.

6 Use a flexible sanding pad to sand the inside of the ring.

7 Decorate and reinforce the seam by creating lines and dots with syringe clay. Let dry. Fire and tumble-polish the ring. Use liver of sulfur to add patina if desired.

For projects that include screen, fire for two hours at a slightly lower temperature (1250°F/677°C) so the screen material doesn't become brittle.

Embellish the ring with beads and crystals

1 Thread the needle with 3–4 ft. (.9–1.2 m) of thread. Tie a knot around a wire in the screen to anchor the thread near the outer edge. Dot the knot with glue to secure.

2 With the needle and thread at the top of the ring, pick up three charlottes, a 4 mm crystal, and another charlotte. Skipping the last charlotte, go back through the crystal, the three charlottes, and the screen.

3 Go up through the next square of the screen, and repeat step 2. Continue until you complete the outer round, and then fill in the center.

4 Tie a knot close to the screen, dot with glue, and bring the thread through one of the beaded strands toward the top. Trim the excess thread.

ariations

Petals with carved details form a beautiful base. Use a clay cutter or create your own free-form shape.

This asymmetrical variation started with a curving, textured leaf band. I added flowing vines made of syringe clay.

bejeweled

Use specialty pliers to set a large gemstone.

This design is an update of a classic look—a single gemstone set in prongs. Elegant leaves frame an oval CZ in fiery orange-red, a brilliant reminder of autumn.

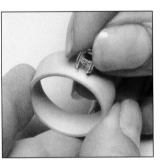

1 To create the shank, follow steps 1–9 of the Autumn Leaves project, p. 26. Place the prong setting in the desired position. Make light dots in the surface of the ring by lightly scratching the surface of the clay with the four feet of the setting.

2 Using a blob of syringe clay, cover a scratched dot.

materials
PMC3 clay (6–8 g)
PMC3 syringe clay
Gemstone, 4 x 6 mm
Fine-silver prong setting,
    4 x 6 mm

tools & supplies
From basic toolkit: balm
    or oil, needle stylus,
    paintbrush, plastic mat,
    sanding pad, ruler, scalpel,
    tweezers
Setting pliers
Mandrel setup: steel ring
    mandrel, sticky note,
    clear tape
Kiln setup
Tumbler setup
Liver of sulfur and polishing
    pad (optional)

This fine-silver prong
setting is made for
use with metal clay.

3 Cover all four dots, making the blobs at least as tall as the feet of the prong setting.

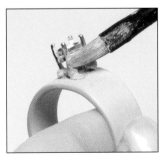

4 Set the prong setting into the blobs. Use the paintbrush to smooth the blobs around the feet of the prong setting. Let dry.

prongs —

feet —

5 To make the leaves: Roll a clay ball about 6–8 mm in diameter and slightly flatten the ball.

6 Pinch both ends with your fingers to make a leaf shape.

7 Press the needle stylus into the clay to create veins.

8 Use a moist paintbrush to smooth the leaf shape.

9 Use syringe clay or paste to attach the leaves on both sides of the setting. Add lines of embellishment with syringe clay. Let dry.

10 Fire and tumble-polish the ring. Use liver of sulfur to add patina if desired.

11 Use setting pliers to set the gemstone (see below).

Using setting pliers to set a gemstone

Hold the setting pliers so that the grooved jaw straddles one prong while the dimple in the other jaw goes to the opposite (diagonal) prong. Grab the prong with the dimpled jaw and gently squeeze. The prong should move slightly.

Change the position of the pliers so the groove straddles the opposite prong (the prong that was just moved by the dimpled jaw) and, again, gently squeeze. Repeat this process with the opposite pair of prongs.

Use your fingers or tweezers to check whether the stone is secure. If not, repeat the process.

variations

Consider stamped, punched, or sculpted images in all shapes and sizes as a base for a prong-set CZ.

moonrise

Paint a natural pod shape with paste clay to create a setting for a pearl.

A pearl nestles within the organic lines of a pod, resembling the moon in the night sky.

1 Put the pod on a toothpick and draw a line around its perimeter with a pencil.

2 Use a paintbrush to paint the lower half of the pod with paste. Let each coat dry thoroughly before you apply the next coat. You will need to paint 8–10 coats. After applying the last coat of paste, let dry thoroughly.

3 To create a smooth top edge, apply a line of syringe clay along the pencil line. Let dry. Fire the clay-coated pod.

4 To create the shank, follow steps 1–9 of the Autumn Leaves project, p. 26.

materials

PMC3 syringe clay
PMC3 paste clay
Natural pod
Half-drilled pearl, about
    8 x 10 mm
22-gauge fine-silver wire,
    ½ in. (13 mm)
Fine-silver casting grain

tools & supplies

From basic toolkit: balm or
    oil, paintbrush, playing
    cards, roller, ruler,
    sanding pad, toothpick
Pencil
Two-part epoxy
Mandrel setup: steel ring
    mandrel, sticky note,
    clear tape
Kiln setup
Tumbler setup
Jewelry tools: chainnose
    pliers, wire cutters
Liver of sulfur and polishing
    pad (optional)

Make sure that any pods you use with metal clay are completely dry and free of chemicals.

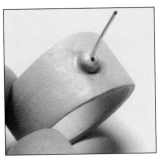

5 Pinch one end of the wire with chainnose pliers to make a small paddle. Make a syringe-clay blob in the center front of the shank.

6 Place the paddle end of the wire into the blob.

7 Place the pod component over the wire and push to adhere it to the shank, letting some syringe clay ooze through the hole. Use a paintbrush to smooth the clay on the inside of the pod.

8 Add syringe clay blobs in gaps at the base of the pod component.

9 Use tweezers to set casting grain in the blobs.

10 If the top edge of the pod component seems rough, apply more syringe clay to cover any sharp parts. Let dry.

11 Fire and tumble-polish the ring. Use liver of sulfur to add patina if desired.

12 Test-fit the pearl on the wire, trimming the wire as needed. Use two-part epoxy to adhere the pearl in place.

A burned-out pod created detail on this ring.

If you use paste over a closed pod shape, only the last layer of paste will show. You won't see any pod texture, so choose an interesting shape.

. water
images

Paint a pattern in wax resist; watch it emerge as you use water to remove clay.

The flowing pattern on this ring suggests a design carved in rock, being slowly smoothed by the endless motion of the ocean's tides.

materials
PMC3 clay (starting
    amount, 25 g; actual
    amount used, 6 g)

tools & supplies
Flat-band RingMaker set,
    8 mm wide
Pencil
Wax resist
Sponge
Cup of water
From basic toolkit: balm or
    oil, plastic mat, sanding
    pad, scalpel
Paintbrush dedicated to
    wax resist
Kiln setup
Tumbler setup
Liver of sulfur and polishing
    pad (optional)

1 To prepare the RingMaker molds, lightly grease the cylinder and the inside of the base, top, and thickness guide. Place the thickness guide over the base.

2 Roll the clay into a ball about 1 in. (26 mm) in diameter.

3 Place the clay into the center of the mold.

4 Place the top of the mold over the clay ball.

5 Press the mold together firmly. Use your fingers to force the clay into all parts of the ring-shaped space.

6 Insert the cylinder in the center of the mold and push down with your finger, holding the mold closed with steady pressure.

7 Push the cylinder all the way through the opening. Remove the plug of clay and preserve for another use.

8 Let the clay dry in the mold at least overnight. Smooth with a flexible sanding pad.

9 Draw a continuous design of waves with a pencil.

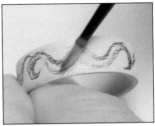

10 Use a paintbrush to coat the design with wax resist. Let dry.

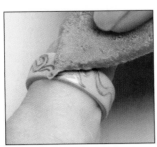

11 Use a wet sponge to gently remove layers of clay from the uncoated portions of the band.

12 Rinse the sponge in a cup of water (you can use the clay that settles to the bottom for paste). Occasionally pause, dry the piece, and check if you're satisfied with the contrast between the raised design and the background. If not, continue removing clay. If any wax resist starts to come off, reapply it and dry the band before continuing.

13 Fire and tumble-polish the ring. Use liver of sulfur to add patina if desired.

A patina helps bring out the contrast in the design.

ariations

Organic shapes and patterns of all kinds are well suited to the water-etching technique.

organic
splendor

Shape this ring shank and cabochon setting entirely from syringe clay.

In this ring, the ocean blue of a dichroic glass cabochon meets the organic lines of syringe clay, which resemble tree roots. Together they convey the balance of earth and water.

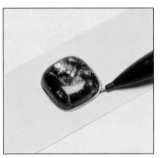

1 Place the dichroic cabochon ("cab" for short) in the center of a sticky note. Trace the outline with a pencil.

2 Wrap the sticky note around the mandrel. Draw a rough outline of the ring on the note and cover it with tape. Use balm or oil to grease the taped surface.

materials
PMC3 syringe clay
Fine-silver casting grain
Dichroic glass cabochon,
   ½ in. (13 mm) square

tools & supplies
From basic toolkit: balm
   or oil, paintbrush, ruler,
   sanding pad, tweezers
Pencil
Mandrel setup: steel ring
   mandrel, sticky note,
   clear tape
Kiln setup
Tumbler setup
Liver of sulfur and polishing
   pad (optional)

3 Using a clay-filled syringe without a tip, place lines of clay over the sketched outline.

4 Build up the cab setting with at least two layers of syringe clay lines. Use a clean, moist paintbrush to shape the clay outline and nudge it into position.

● You may use as much as two-thirds of a syringe in
● this project, so be sure you have enough on hand.
●

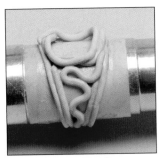

5 Continue to use the syringe without the tip to add lines of embellishment to the sides of the shank.

6 Place the cab in the setting. Add an L-shaped reinforcement on two opposite corners and frame the cab with additional lines of clay. Use a moist paintbrush to smooth the syringe clay lines.

7 Using a syringe with a tip, make a clay blob on the shank as shown.

8 Set casting grain in the blob with tweezers. Fill any open spaces with casting grain set in clay blobs as desired. Let the ring dry on the mandrel.

9 Remove from the mandrel. Use syringe clay to fill any gaps inside the ring and smooth it out with a paintbrush. Let dry. Sand the inside with a flexible sanding pad.

10 Fire and tumble-polish the ring. Use liver of sulfur to add patina if desired.

● Fire projects that contain glass at a low temperature (1250°F/677°C).
● Let the kiln cool to room temperature before removing.
●

variations

This variation features shapely lines of syringe clay over a flat band.

Here's another dichroic cab encased in syringe clay to create a pendant. A few small CZs add sparkle.

waves

You'll gain skill in shaping and joining smooth snakes as you build this ring.

Capture the primal power of a wave in this ring. Carry the theme through with a deep blue CZ at its center.

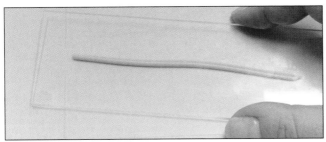

1 Prepare the mandrel. Roll a clay snake about 5 in. (13 cm) long.

materials
PMC3 clay (6–8 g)
PMC3 syringe clay
PMC3 paste clay (optional)
CZ or lab-created corundum,
  4 mm

tools & supplies
From basic toolkit: balm
  or oil, paintbrush, plastic
  mat, rolling rectangle,
  ruler, sanding pad, scalpel,
  tweezers
Mandrel setup: steel ring
  mandrel, sticky note,
  clear tape
Kiln setup
Tumbler setup
Liver of sulfur and polishing
  pad (optional)

2 Shape the snake in a coil on and around the mandrel as shown. Attach the end of the snake to the coil with syringe clay.

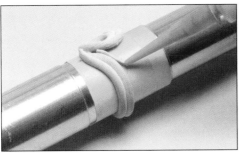

3 Roll another snake about 3 in. (76 mm) long. Lay it alongside the first and attach using paste or syringe clay. Trim the excess clay. Add a line of syringe clay along the second snake.

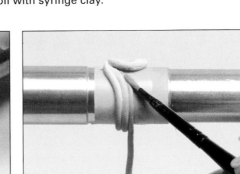

4 Roll another snake. Lay this snake alongside the second and attach it. Use the paintbrush to smooth the snake into position. Trim the excess clay.

5 Let the ring dry on the mandrel. Remove it from the mandrel and carefully sand it with a flexible sanding pad.

6 Use syringe clay to fill any gaps inside the ring.

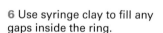

7 Smooth with a paintbrush. Let dry.

8 Sand the inside of the ring with a flexible sanding pad. Place it back on the prepared spot on the mandrel.

9 Moisten the center of the coil.

10 In the center of the coil, make a syringe-clay blob that's at least 5 mm.

11 Using tweezers, gently set the stone onto the blob.

12 Push it into the blob until the girdle (widest part) of the stone sinks below the surface of the clay. Let dry.

13 Sand if necessary to smooth the surface. Fire and tumble-polish the ring. Use liver of sulfur to add patina if desired.

ariations

Clay snakes are a strong, dense alternative to using syringe clay to frame a cabochon or embellish a vessel.

shadow box

Learn how to wet-pack enamels as you add colorful depth to this ring.

A Polynesian-inspired stamp design filled with cool enamel colors is the focal point of this ring.

1 Prepare the mandrel. Roll the clay to 5 cards (1.25 mm) thick, at least 4 in. (10 cm) long, and about ⅝ in. (16 mm) wide.

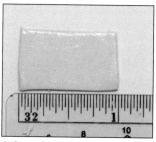

2 Cut a 1-in. (26 mm) segment from the rolled clay.

3 Place the segment on the prepared mandrel. (This segment adds the depth needed for creating a flat surface in step 7.)

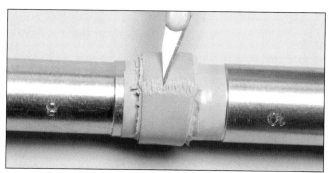

4 Wrap the remaining strip of clay around the mandrel and over the segment so the ends overlap at the center point of the segment. Trim the ends at that center point and remove the excess clay. Gently lift the ends and apply syringe clay to adhere the top strip to the segment underneath. Lightly scrape the seam with the scalpel to merge the ends and strengthen the seam.

● ●● ●●
materials
PMC3 clay (12–16 g)
Syringe clay

tools & supplies
From basic toolkit: balm or oil, paintbrush, plastic mat, playing cards, roller, ruler, sanding pad, scalpel
Square clay cutters, two sizes
Texture sheet
Enamels in two cool colors
Plastic spoons
Paintbrush dedicated to enamels
Eyedropper or mister
Dust mask
Mandrel setup: steel ring mandrel, sticky note, clear tape
Kiln setup
Tumbler setup
Liver of sulfur and polishing pad (optional)

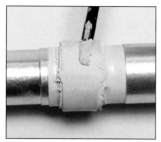

5 Add more syringe clay along the seam and smooth with the paintbrush.

6 Examine the ring from this view. If you see any gaps, fill them with syringe clay. Let dry on the mandrel.

7 Use a sanding pad to create a flat spot on the thick part of the shank.

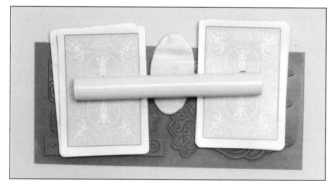

8 Roll the remaining clay to 7 cards (1.75 mm) thick. Roll the clay on a stamp sheet to 6 cards (1.5 mm) thick.

9 Use a clay cutter to punch a square from the textured clay.

10 Roll the excess clay to 4 cards (1 mm) thick. Punch a square using the same size clay cutter, then use the smaller cutter to punch another square, creating a frame. Remove the inside square. Let the textured square and the frame dry.

11 Use a sanding pad to smooth the edges of all three pieces.

12 Apply syringe clay around the perimeter of the textured square.

13 Layer the frame over the textured square. Let the piece dry. Smooth all of the edges with a sanding pad.

14 Apply syringe clay to several spots on the ring shank and attach the frame component.

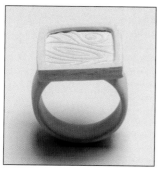

15 Let the ring dry. Fire and tumble-polish the ring.

16 Put a small amount of each enamel color into a teaspoon. Add a few drops of water.

17 Using the paintbrush, pick up a small amount of enamel and pack it into the framed area. Fill the entire area within the frame with a thin layer of enamel. If the enamel starts to dry before you finish, add a few drops of water with an eyedropper or mister.

Always wear a dust mask when handling dry enamels.

18 Prop the ring so the enameled area is level (vermiculite in a small clay saucer works well for this). Fire for 2–3 minutes at 1450°F (788°C). Polish again.

If you like, fill in open spots or add another layer to deepen the color. Simply add enamel and refire until you are satisfied with the results.

variations

With the RIngMaker mold, you can create a bezeled setting that is perfect for holding layers of enamel.

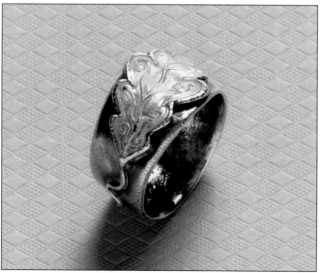

Any stamped image with a raised outline, like this oak leaf, makes a good surface for enameling.

elegant solitaire

Build a tall setting with syringe-clay prongs to hold a large lab-created gemstone.

This commanding setting is fit for a monarch, yet the clay-dot prongs keep things a bit playful.

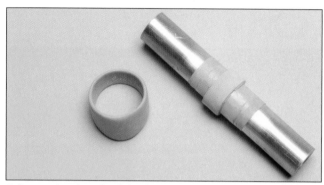

1 Create the ring shank by following steps 1–9 of the Autumn Leaves project, p. 26. Make the top of the shank wide enough to accommodate the setting you'll make next. Use a smaller mandrel to create a second band to use as the setting for the stone. Make this band at least 5 mm wide and an even width—a simple band, not an hourglass shape. Let both pieces dry on the mandrels.

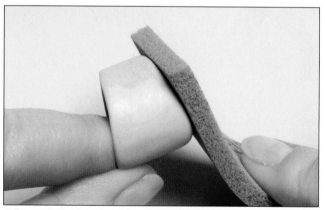

2 Smooth the bands with a sanding pad.

materials
PMC3 clay (12–16 g)
PMC3 syringe clay
Round CZ or lab-created
  gemstone, 14 mm

tools & supplies
Mandrel for stone setting
  (see tip below)
From basic toolkit: balm or
  oil, paintbrush, plastic
  mat, playing cards, roller,
  ruler, sanding pad, scalpel,
  tweezers
Half-round sanding stick
Mandrel setup: steel ring
  mandrel, sticky note,
  clear tape
Kiln setup
Tumbler setup
Liver of sulfur and polishing
  pad (optional)

The mandrel for the stone setting should have a circumference of about 12 mm. Anything round that's the right size, such as a thick felt-tipped marker, will work.

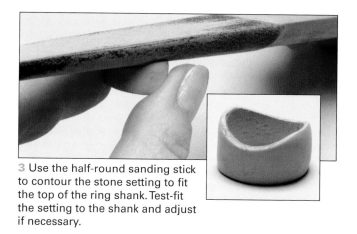

3 Use the half-round sanding stick to contour the stone setting to fit the top of the ring shank. Test-fit the setting to the shank and adjust if necessary.

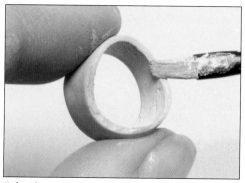

4 Apply paste or syringe clay to the setting where it will touch the shank. Place the setting on the shank.

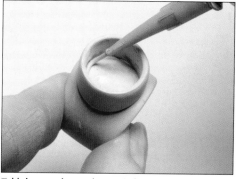

5 Using syringe clay, reinforce the join on the inside of the setting.

6 With a paintbrush, remove excess clay and smooth the join.

7 Reinforce the outside of the join with a line of syringe clay.

8 With a paintbrush, remove excess clay. Smooth.

9 Make a syringe clay dot on at the base of the setting.

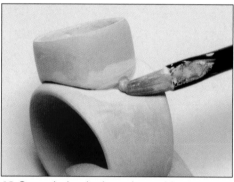

10 Smooth the dot into place with a moist paintbrush. Make a total of eight dots, spaced equally apart.

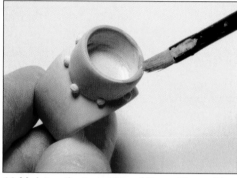

11 Moisten the top edge of the setting with the paintbrush. This will help keep the stone in place.

12 Place the stone in the setting. Using the dots you made earlier as a guide, place eight dots of syringe clay around the top edge. Let the ring dry.

13 Fire and tumble-polish the ring. Use liver of sulfur to add patina if desired.

ariations

I used a square dowel to shape the setting for this lab-made stone.

I like using stamped images as backgrounds for elegant solitaires.

whimsical framed gem

This technique uses structural elements that are flexible enough to conform to large CZs of nearly any shape.

Windswept leaves and branches encircle the gemstone of this ring.

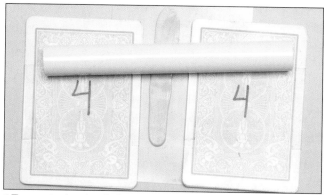

1 To create the shank, follow steps 1–9 of the Autumn Leaves project, p. 26. To create the CZ setting, roll the clay into a strip 4 cards (1 mm) thick and about 3 in. (76 mm) long.

follow steps 1–9 of the Autumn Leaves project, p. 26.

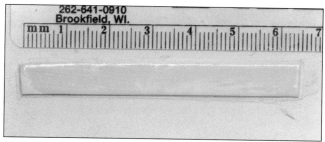

2 Trim the clay to about 2½ x ¼ in. (64 x 7 mm).

materials
PMC3 clay (12–16 g)
PMC3 syringe clay
PMC sheet clay, ½ sheet
Laser-cut CZ, 15 mm square

tools & supplies
From basic toolkit: balm
  or oil, paintbrush,
  plastic mat, playing cards,
  roller, ruler, sanding pad,
  scalpel, tweezers
Craft punch, leaf shape
Square dowel, ⅜ in. (10 mm)
Elmer's glue
Half-round sanding stick
Mandrel setup: steel ring
  mandrel, sticky note,
  clear tape
Kiln setup
Tumbler setup
Liver of sulfur and polishing
  pad (optional)

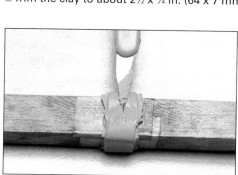

3 Prepare the square dowel with a sticky note and greased tape. Form the clay strip around the dowel, joining the ends. Blend the seam with the scalpel.

4 Smooth with the paintbrush. Let dry on the dowel.

5 To create a thicker piece of sheet clay for the leaf prongs, fold it in half and add a thin layer of glue. After the glue dries, use the craft punch to create four leaf shapes.

6 Use the glue to attach the leaf shapes to the CZ as shown. Attach them only to the top of the CZ; the other parts of the leaf shapes will be loose until step 9.

7 Use the half-round sanding stick to contour the setting to fit the shank.

8 Use syringe clay to attach the setting to the ring. Apply additional syringe clay within the setting to reinforce the join.

9 Spread and smooth the clay with the paintbrush.

10 Secure the CZ in the setting by gluing the leaf shapes to the setting. Reinforce with decorative lines of syringe clay over the stone and on the setting.

11 Let the ring dry. Fire, tumble-polish, and use liver of sulfur to add patina if desired.

● I used a small craft punch in a style
● called "Deco Leaf." It punches a leaf
● shape about ⅝ in. (16 mm) long.

ariations

Punched shapes are a decorative alternative to standard prongs. This technique works best if the CZ is at least 8 mm.

classic
bezel

In this project, you'll use a small butane torch to fuse fine-silver bezel wire.
The gemstone is added after firing, so choose any type of stone you like.

For this classic-looking ring design, I chose a kyanite gemstone that's as vibrant as a blue jay.

• • •

materials
PMC3 clay (12–16 g)
PMC3 syringe clay or paste
Art Clay oil paste
2½ in. (64 mm) fine-silver
   bezel wire, ⅛ in. (3 mm)
   wide
Cabochon, 15 mm square

tools & supplies
From basic toolkit: balm or
   oil, paintbrush, plastic
   mat, playing cards, roller,
   ruler, sanding pad, scalpel
Square clay cutter, 1 in.
   (26 mm)
Paintbrush dedicated to
   oil paste
Butane torch
Firebrick or kiln shelf
Wire cutters
Bezel pusher
Mandrel setup: steel ring
   mandrel, sticky note,
   clear tape
Kiln setup
Tumbler setup
Liver of sulfur and polishing
   pad (optional)
Two-part epoxy (optional)

1 To create the shank, follow steps 1–7 of the Shadow Box project, p. 56. Roll the excess clay to 4 cards (1 mm) thick. Use the clay cutter to punch a square. Let dry.

2 Contour the sides of the flat square piece as shown to make a platform.

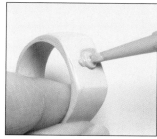

3 Attach the platform to the ring shank with syringe clay or paste.

4 Let the ring dry. Fire it, but do not polish.

- Fine-silver wire will fuse without solder. Be sure the ends are cut flush and perfectly aligned before fusing.

5 To shape the bezel, wrap the bezel wire around the cabochon. Use wire cutters to cut the wire so the ends are flush. Use the torch to fuse the ends: Place the shaped wire on the firebrick or kiln shelf, turn on the torch, and keep the flame moving to heat the entire wire to a warm orange glow. Watch for the silver to glisten to indicate that it has fused.

6 Use oil paste to attach the bezel to the platform of the fired ring.

7 Add a line of syringe clay to reinforce the join. Let the ring dry overnight.

8 Fire and tumble-polish the ring. Use liver of sulfur to add patina if desired.

9 Test-fit the stone. Use a layer of two-part epoxy, if desired, to secure the stone. Push the bezel wire over the stone with a bezel pusher (a square wooden dowel works well).

ariations

With this technique, you can make a bezel for a gemstone of any size and shape. Because the stone is added after firing, you don't have to worry about it withstanding high temperatures. Consider embellishing the platform with syringe clay and CZs.

Carry the platform idea further with shapes, sizes, and texture. In this design, I used two different triangular platforms.

suspended
gem

This technique gives a nod to traditional channel-setting methods.

This ring suggests an all-seeing eye, a protective symbol in many cultures. Make it and wear it in good health!

1 To create the shank, follow steps 1–6 of the Autumn Leaves project, p. 26. While the shank is wet, make an incision in the center about ⅝ in. (16 mm) long.

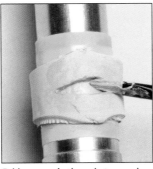

2 Use a paintbrush to push the two sides apart. Let dry on the mandrel. Use a sanding pad to smooth all parts of the shank, including inside the incision.

materials
PMC3 clay (12–16 g)
PMC3 syringe clay or paste
CZ, 7 x 5 mm

tools & supplies
Fern stamp
From basic toolkit: balm or oil, paintbrush, plastic mat, playing cards, roller, ruler, sanding pad, scalpel, tweezers
Round file
Mandrel setup: steel ring mandrel, sticky note, clear tape
Kiln setup
Tumbler setup
Liver of sulfur and polishing pad (optional)

3 Roll the remaining clay to 8 cards (2 mm) thick and about 1½ in. (38 mm) long.

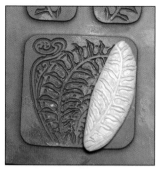

4 Press the clay onto the stamp with your fingers.

5 Flex the ruler to trim the clay into a long leaf shape.

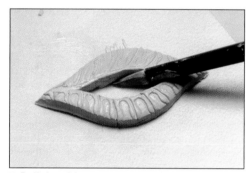

6 Make an incision in the center of the leaf component (don't go all the way to the ends).

7 Pull the sides apart, creating an opening.

8 Attach the component to the shank with paste or syringe. Let dry.

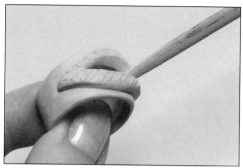

9 Use a round file to enlarge the opening until it's nearly large enough to hold the stone.

10 Smooth the entire ring with a sanding pad.

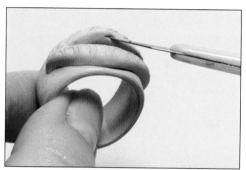

11 Using the scalpel, create grooves on the top and bottom of the opening, about 1 mm from the outside surface.

12 Gently fit the stone into the grooves.

13 Fire and tumble-polish the ring. Use liver of sulfur to add patina if desired.

variations

Here's a smooth approach to the same design. I accented the setting with lines of syringe clay.

Capture a CZ in the center of a flowing leaf pendant.

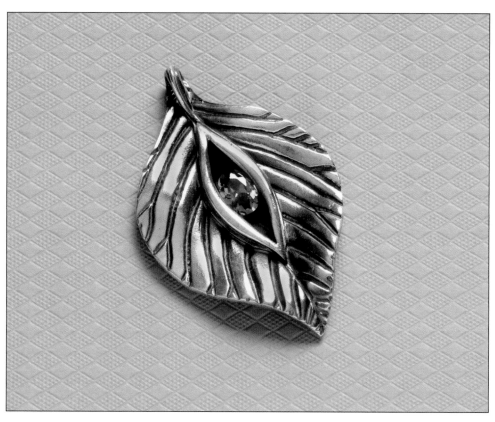

spinner

This focal bead is formed with metal clay paste over cork clay. It spins on a thin, hand-rolled metal clay rod.

This celestial-themed ring is always in motion.

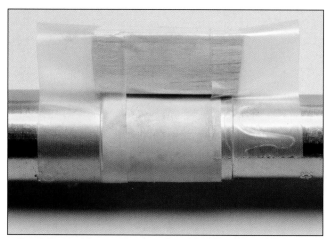

1 Prepare the ring mandrel as usual. Wrap tape around a square dowel. Tape the rod to the mandrel on each of its ends. Apply balm or oil to the center pieces of tape where the clay will be wrapped.

2 Roll the clay to 5 cards (1.25 mm) thick and at least 3½ in. (89 mm) long. Trim to about ⅜ in. (10 mm) wide.

● ● ●

materials
PMC3 clay (8–12 g)
PMC3 syringe clay
PMC3 paste
Fine-silver casting grain

tools & supplies
Cork clay
Square dowel, ⅜ in. (10 mm)
Wood skewer
Texture sheet
Clay cutters
From basic toolkit: balm
    or oil, paintbrush, plastic
    mat, playing cards, roller,
    rolling rectangle, ruler,
    sanding pad, scalpel,
    tweezers
Mandrel setup: steel ring
    mandrel, sticky note,
    clear tape
Kiln setup
Tumbler setup
Liver of sulfur and polishing
    pad (optional)

● If you like, you can
● substitute a porcelain
● bead blank for the
   cork clay sphere.

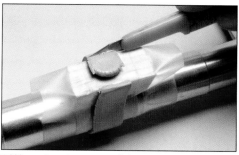

3 Wrap the clay around the mandrel so the ends extend to the top of the dowel rod. Trim the ends where they overlap the corners as shown. Let the shank dry on the mandrel.

4 Smooth with a flexible sanding pad. Round all four corners.

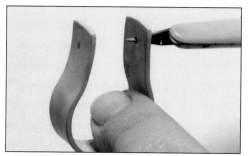

5 Rotate the scalpel point to create a hole about 2 mm wide on each side as shown.

6 Shape cork clay into a ½-in. (13 mm) sphere and put it on a skewer. Let the form dry, then loosen it on the skewer to make sure it is removable. Use a paintbrush to cover the form with paste. Paint 8–10 coats, letting each coat dry thoroughly before you apply the next coat. Let the piece dry thoroughly.

7 Roll the remaining clay to 2 cards (.5 mm) thick.

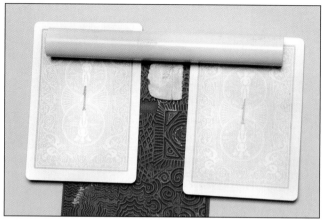

8 Roll the clay to 1 card (.25 mm) thick on a stamp sheet.

9 Punch out shapes with clay cutters.

10 Attach the shapes to the bead using thin paste.

11 Use syringe clay to embellish the bead around the openings.

12 Smooth the syringe embellishment with a paintbrush.

13 Use the rolling rectangle to roll a thin snake. This will become the rod that the bead rotates on, so make it slender enough to fit inside the bead—about the thickness of the toothpick. Let dry.

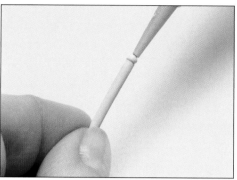

14 Smooth the rod with a sanding pad. Trim it so it is just long enough to fit through the bead and the ring shank. Make a syringe-clay blob on one end.

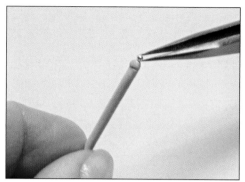

15 Set a silver casting grain in the blob. Let the piece dry.

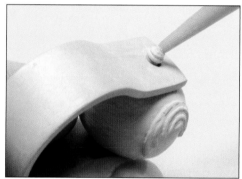

16 Insert the rod through the holes in the ring shank and the bead. Make a syringe blob on the opposite end of the rod.

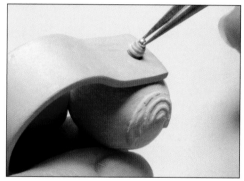

17 Set another casting grain. Add more syringe-clay embellishment to the shank if desired and let the piece dry.

18 Fire and tumble-polish the ring. Use liver of sulfur to add patina if desired.

variations

I made a variety of free-form spacers and carved their sides for this kinetic pendant.

The spinner setting lends an unexpected twist to a classic single pearl. After firing the setting, I added the pearl on 18-gauge sterling silver wire.

sanctuary

*Put your construction skills to the test as you build a tiny cottage
from metal clay and mount it to the ring shank.*

I love to travel. I've seen many fascinating buildings, large and small, throughout the world. I tried to capture some unusual architectural elements in this tiny sanctuary to wear on your hand.

1 To create the ring shank, follow steps 1–7 of the Shadow Box project, p. 56. Make the shank large enough to hold the structure you'll build in the following steps.

2 To make the roof, mix two-part molding compound and press the CZ point-first into the mold.

● ● ●
materials
PMC3 clay (16–20 g)
PMC3 syringe clay
Laser-cut CZ, 15 mm square

tools & supplies
From basic toolkit: balm
   or oil, needle stylus,
   paintbrush, plastic mat,
   playing cards, roller, ruler,
   sanding pad, scalpel
Square clay cutter, ¾ in.
   (19 mm)
Paper
Pencil
Wood form, ½ x ½ x ⅝ in.
   (13 x 13 x 16 mm)
Two-part molding compound
Texture sheet
Round file
Elmer's glue
Fine-silver casting grain
Mandrel setup: steel ring
   mandrel, sticky note,
   clear tape
Kiln setup
Tumbler setup
Liver of sulfur and polishing
   pad (optional)
Two-part epoxy (optional)

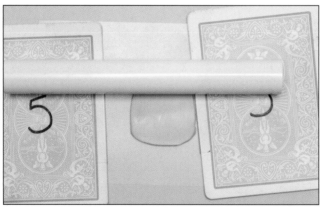

3 Roll the remaining clay into a square slightly bigger than the clay cutter and 6 cards (1.5 mm) thick.

● This CZ has the look of a tiled
● roof. I used it to create a mold
● for my structure.

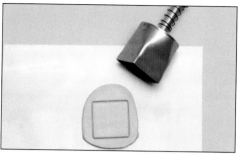

4 Use the clay cutter to punch a square in the clay.

5 Press the clay into the mold. Let dry.

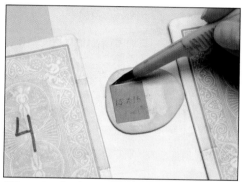

6 To make the front and back panels: Make a paper stencil that is 15 x 16 mm. Roll the clay to 4 cards (1 mm) thick. Place the stencil on the clay and trim around it with the scalpel. Make a second clay rectangle and set both aside to dry.

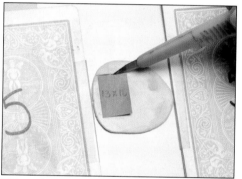

7 To make the textured sides: Make a paper stencil that is 13 x 16 mm. Roll the clay to 5 cards (1.25 mm) thick. Cut two rectangles from the clay using the second stencil. Do not let them dry; go on to step 8.

8 Roll the second pair of rectangles on a stamp sheet to 4 cards (1 mm) thick.

9 Let the textured pair of rectangles dry.

10 Smooth the edges of all the rectangles with a sanding pad.

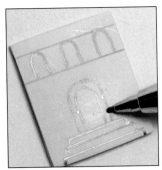

11 With a pencil, draw doors, windows, steps, and other details on the front and back panels.

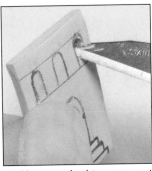

12 Use a scalpel to carve out the window openings.

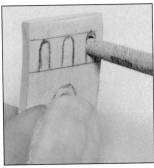

13 Use the round file to smooth the tops of the openings.

14 Use a needle stylus to scribe the other details into the clay.

15 To attach the front panel, apply glue to one side of the wood form.

16 Place the front panel on the wood form. Attach the back on the opposite side of the wood form in the same way. Test-fit the sides. Adjust by sanding if necessary.

17 Use a line of syringe clay at each corner to join the sides to the front and back panels.

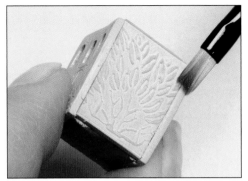

18 Smooth the seams with a paintbrush.

19 Apply lines of syringe clay along the top edge.

20 Attach the roof, smoothing the clay if necessary.

21 Attach the sanctuary to the ring shank with syringe clay.

22 Add a line of syringe clay along the bottom of the sanctuary, and place a piece of casting grain at each corner. Repeat along the base of the roof. Let dry.

23 Fire and tumble-polish the ring. Use liver of sulfur to add patina if desired.

● The square wood
● form will burn away
● during firing.

variations

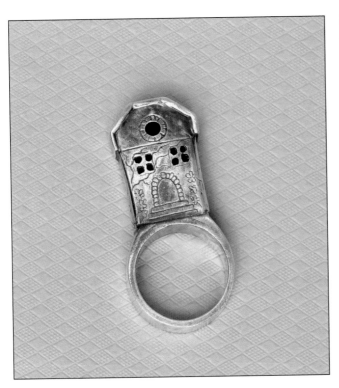

Nearly any type of simple structure can be shaped into a Sanctuary ring.

The roof mold can be used to shape a pendant or earring components.

metal clay
basics

Materials, tools, and techniques

Metal clay is almost magical. In its moist form, small metal particles are suspended in an organic binder. When fired, the binder burns away to leave only solid metal.

Silver metal clay, which is used for all the projects in this book, is available as lump clay, syringe clay, paste, and sheet clay. Two brands of silver clay are available—Precious Metal Clay (PMC) and Art Clay. Products in both lines have similar properties and are packaged with complete firing directions.

The newest generation of clays, PMC3 and ACS 650, can be fired at lower temperatures if desired. Low-fire clay is best for making rings because it is denser than other clay formulas and can withstand heavy wear.

Clay types
Lump clay can be rolled into sheets or snakes, textured, sculpted, or shaped by hand. Lump clay contains a low proportion of water and can dry out quickly.

Syringe clay is watered-down metal clay in a syringe applicator. Use syringe clay to adhere pieces together, seal seams, set stones and casting grain, and create lines, dots, and other shapes.

Metal clay paste has the consistency of thick paint. Paste can be purchased, or you can make your own by adding a bit of water to leftover bits of unfired metal clay and clay dust. Paste can be painted onto bisque beads, organic items, or cork clay. Thinned paste, often called "slip," is used to join pieces of unfired clay.

Sheet or paper-type clay is oil-based; it doesn't dry out as you work. It can be folded like paper, cut with scissors, or used with craft punches to form intricate shapes. Sheet clay does not stick to itself; use paste clay or Elmer's glue to laminate pieces of sheet clay together.

Use **oil paste** to adhere shapes together and to make repairs. It's especially effective on fired pieces or for attaching fine-silver components such as a bezel or wire. (You can find instructions for making oil paste using lavender oil online.)

Additional materials
What else can you use to create metal clay jewelry? Silver wire, findings, and a stash of beautiful beads, pearls, and crystals.

Use **fine-silver wire** when adding wire to silver clay before firing. Like the clay, it is pure silver and doesn't oxidize in the kiln. But because it is pure, it's also softer than sterling silver, so using a tumbler or magnetic polisher to harden the piece after firing is a good idea.

Use fine-silver **casting grain** to add detail to silver clay pieces. You can make your own by balling up scrap pieces of fine-silver wire with a torch.

Choose **CZs** or lab-grown stones that are **kiln-safe** if these will be fired within your metal clay items.

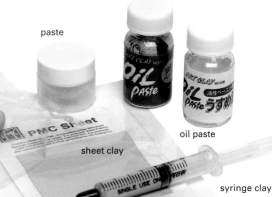

paste

lump clay

sheet clay

oil paste

syringe clay

Basic tools

You'll use these tools for shaping nearly every metal clay project. If you're just starting out, this is a good toolkit to assemble.

Any surface that touches metal clay must be lightly greased. This includes the work surface, roller, and any miscellaneous tools such as the RingMaker mold or straws for making bails. A **natural hand balm** or olive oil works well.

Use a **paintbrush** to apply slip. I like a brush with a small, short tip called a *bright*. Always keep a small **cup of water** nearby. Moisten the paintbrush for shaping and smoothing. Use it dry to brush clay debris off sanded pieces.

Use a **needle stylus** to make or mark holes. It also works well for signing your pieces before firing.

Keep some **paper towels** handy at all times. Use a towel to wipe your paintbrush and to wick away excess water on your work. Touch a corner of the towel to the wet portion and the water will soak upward; avoid wiping the wet piece.

Create **plastic work mats** by cutting apart clear report covers or flexible Teflon baking sheets. Lightly grease the mat before working on it. If the mat becomes scored, switch to a new mat to avoid marring your work.

Use **playing cards** or measuring slats to control the thickness of rolled clay. Tape cards together to make sets of 2, 3, 4, 5, and 6. In some cases you may want a single-card thickness.

Used to flatten metal clay to a specific thickness, a **roller** may be a length of narrow

PVC pipe or an acrylic rod. Always grease the roller lightly before use.

A **rolling rectangle** is a piece of clear plastic used to roll clay into smooth, uniform cylinders referred to as "snakes."

Use a **small, clear ruler** that measures millimeters and inches. Beads are usually sized in millimeters.

Use a **scalpel** or craft knife for cutting clay and making small holes.

Use **straws** of various diameters to punch holes in clay and to create bails.

Use **tweezers** to pick up and set CZs and casting grain, and to remove leaves and stems after imprinting them.

Keep a **small mister** (spray bottle) or an eyedropper handy for hydrating clay.

92

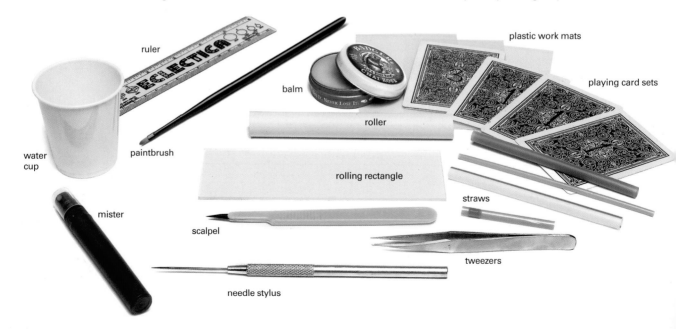

ruler

plastic work mats

balm

playing card sets

roller

water cup

paintbrush

rolling rectangle

straws

mister

scalpel

tweezers

needle stylus

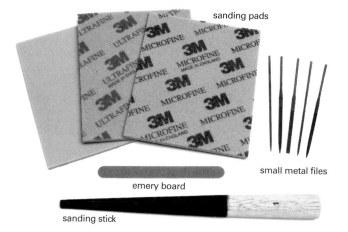

sanding pads

small metal files

emery board

sanding stick

polishing pads

polishing cloth

agate burnishers

wire brush

liver of sulfur

Abrasive tools

Use flexible **sanding pads** to smooth dimensional pieces after they are dry. An **emery board** is handy for filing flat edges and surfaces.

Full- and half-round sanding sticks are used to sand the inside of curved surfaces such as rings. They are available in different grits and are often sold in sets.

Use **metal files** to file irregularly shaped pieces or to get into crevices that an emery board or flexible sanding pad just can't reach. I suggest you keep two sets handy: small and extra-small.

Finishing tools and supplies

Agate burnishers give a bright polish to high spots on fired silver. A burnisher also can be used as a bezel pusher.

Liver of sulfur adds a patina or an antique finish to fired pieces. It's available in lump, liquid, or gel form.

If you add patina, use **polishing pads** to leave color only in the low spots of the silver.

Polishing cloths give a final shine to any fired piece, whether a patina has been applied or not. No polishing compound is necessary.

If you don't have access to a tumbler or magnetic polisher, use a **wire brush** to polish fired pieces.

Specialty supplies

Wax resist and a **small sponge** are used for water etching. Use a pencil to sketch onto dry clay, then use a small paintbrush to paint wax resist over the lines. When dry, gently sponge off layers of clay.

To texture moist clay, use **texture sheets** or stamps made of acrylic, brass, or rubber.

For enameling, choose **lead-free enamels** in cool colors if you're a beginner.

Punch shapes out of clay with **clay cutters** and **craft punches**.

Mix equal amounts of **two-part molding** compound to a uniform color, then impress an object to get a reusable mold.

Use **toothpicks** or wood skewers to punch holes or form small bails.

wax resist and sponge

enamels

two-part molding compound

craft punch and clay cutters

toothpicks

texture sheets

Drying

Metal clay needs to be completely dry before it can be fired; otherwise, moisture in the clay will cause cracks or breaks.

Let pieces dry overnight, or speed drying time by using low heat from a drying appliance such as a mug warmer or a griddle set to the lowest possible temperature (about 150°F/66°C). Turn flat pieces over occasionally as they dry. On a warm surface, most pieces will dry within 20–25 minutes. Look for a uniform light color—dark areas indicate moisture, which can cause cracks.

For dimensional pieces, use a food dehydrator. Thorough drying may take 30 minutes or more. A dehydrator is also good for drying leaves and seed pods before covering them with paste.

Kiln firing

For maximum strength and durability, metal clay rings should be fired at 1650°F (900°C) for two hours, whenever possible (as long as the project directions do not call for firing at a lower temperature). A small, digitally programmable electric kiln is the best way to hold this temperature for that length of time. Place items on a kiln shelf. Always use tongs if you are placing items into a preheated kiln and to remove items from a hot kiln.

Polishing

When silver clay is fired, the surface appears white. Polishing smooths the reflective particles in the metal, revealing a shiny silver surface.

To polish, brush the fired piece with a wire brush and soapy water. Rubbing the silver firmly with an agate burnisher will create a high shine. For fast results and a work-hardened, durable ring, tumble the piece for a few hours in a rotary tumbler with stainless steel shot, burnishing compound, and water, or use a magnetic polisher.

Keeping clay moist

Metal clay in lump form dries out very quickly. Remove only what you need from the package, and wrap any excess clay in plastic wrap. Use a mister to spritz the clay from time to time as you're working with it.

To keep syringe clay fresh while working, place it tip-down in a cup of water. For longer-term storage, a florist's water tube works great.

A programmable kiln can hold precise temperatures for set lengths of time.

Use a rotary tumbler to work-harden and polish your rings.

Rolling metal clay

Lightly grease a plastic mat and roller, and place the clay on the mat between two equal stacks of cards. Rest the ends of the roller on the cards to make sure the clay is evenly rolled.

Handling and sanding

Once the clay has dried, it can be fragile. Work gently and carefully when filing, adding holes, and sanding. Do all of your sanding before firing the piece; dry, unfired clay is much easier to sand than fired clay. Pay special attention to sanding the insides of rings to make them smooth. You can collect the sanding dust and make it into slip by adding water, or add it to paste of the same type.

Kiln-safe materials

CZs and synthetic corundums can withstand any recommended firing temperature for silver clay. Dichroic glass can be fired in the kiln with low-fire silver clay. Most glass begins to flow at 1400°F (760°C), so it is not recommended that you use high-fire silver clay products with glass.

Adding your signature

To add initials or your signature before firing, use a needle stylus to lightly scratch the surface. Retrace the lines, removing a small amount of clay.

Adding a patina

After silver clay is fired, use a liver of sulfur solution to add a colorful sheen to the surface. Use tweezers to dip the piece. When the silver is a color you like, remove it and rinse with cold water. Use a polishing pad to remove some of the patina from the raised areas.

about the author

Irina Miech has been involved in the jewelry world for more than 20 years. She owns the retail bead store Eclectica, and she offers instruction in wirework, beading, and metal clay techniques through her Bead Studio.

This is Irina's fifth book for Kalmbach Books. She has authored three additional books of metal clay jewelry projects and is also the author of Beautiful Wire Jewelry for Beaders. Irina also contributes projects to Bead&Button, BeadStyle, Art Jewelry, and other publications.

Irina is a graduate of the University of Wisconsin–Milwaukee. She lives with her husband and sons in southeastern Wisconsin.

acknowledgments

I would like to thank my husband, Tony Miech, for his unwavering support of my work; Lauren Walsh for her writing advice; and my sons, Zachary and David, for their inspirational encouragement and love.

I thank my editor, Mary Wohlgemuth, and the rest of the Kalmbach staff for their invaluable assistance.

I also give thanks to my wonderful store staff for all of their enthusiastic help and continual support.

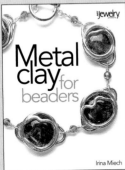